June 16, 2015

OPEN, ACTIVATE & INSPIRE YOUR LIFESPATH™

Dear Wei,

You started me on my lifespath w/ meditation & self-love! XOXO, Juliette

THE FOUR TENETS OF
LOVE

JULIETTE TAYLOR-DE VRIES

Published by Flower of Life Press™
www.FlowerofLifePress.com

Editor:
Scott Watrous, www.FlowerofLifePress.com

Design and Art Direction:
Jane Ashley, www.FlowerofLifePress.com

Photos by Shutterstock.com

TABLE OF CONTENTS

DEDICATION

To *you*. May you live with passion, purpose and love on your LifesPath™.

May my word be one with my thought,
And my thought
Be one with my word. O Lord of Love,
Let me realize you in my consciousness.
May I realize the truth of the scriptures
And translate it into my daily life.
May I proclaim the truth of the scriptures.
May I speak the truth. May it protect me,
And may it protect my teacher.

~*OM shanti shanti shanti (The Upanishads)*[1]

To my mom, **Elsebeth Lauge Grue,** "The Duchess" who taught me to always follow my heart, to show up with truth and authenticity to the world, and to never stand down.

To all the Goddesses here and through the mists of time who remind us of who we really are—divine.

ACKNOWLEDGMENTS

It is with deepest gratitude and love that I want to thank each and every person that has touched my life for they have made me who I am today.

I would like to acknowledge and express my deepest gratitude and thankfulness for the following people:

To **Scott Watrous** and **Jane Ashley** of Flower of Life Press™. Scott, thank you for being the fire in my belly and for bringing order to my thoughts, channeling my messages and connecting with me in the ethereal. Your magic spreads seeds of inspiration and fairy dust.

Jane, thank you for breathing my words to life like a maestro using symbols, color and storylines—building notes of beauty resonating on the page. You are a magician and the muse in my heart.

Scott and Jane, without you both, I would have never have finished this book nor explored the deeper depths of my soul.

For what is inside of you is what is outside of you,
and the one who fashions you on the
outside is the one who shaped the inside of you.
And what you see outside of you, you see inside
of you; it is visible and it is your garment.

~THE NAG HAMMADI LIBRARY, THE THUNDER [2]

ACKNOWLEDGMENTS

To **Razonia McClellan** who has been with me through thick and thin and through good times and bad. She embraced me for my drama, my faults, and my desire to live as life presented itself. She is my sounding board, my revelation, and my truth.

To all the **teachers** past, present and future opening the doors of my imagination and leading me through the rabbit hole with skill and determination. I am another person because of them. **Mrs. Katchetorian**, my world language arts teacher, lives in eternity and her words ring true then as now. "Open your world to writing the stories of your soul."

To my father **Lawrence Cade** for his honesty, and for opening my reality, and to his wife Dilia for her constant support and for enduring our drive down the Coast from Big Sur to San Diego, insisting on stopping at Henry Miller's pad for reflection and rejuvenation.

To my sister **Lela Cade** whose strength and determination rival any warrior, and who spent hours from Italy Skyping words of encouragement and remembrances of old family shenanigans, bringing light and laughter.

To my furry boys, **Benny and Clyde,** who walked with me everyday knowing it was my reprieve and my solace. They knew that rain or shine the walk was a needed act to bring these words forth.

To my children **Dagen, Redmayne,** and **Alexandria:** You embody unconditional love and show me every-day how much you love me, and I get to show you how much I love and admire each and every one of you.

I wish to acknowledge all whom I may not have mentioned by name and that have been a pivotal part of my growth and evolution to this place of birthing this book.

Love is the cure, for your pain
will keep giving birth to more
pain until your eyes constantly
exhale love as effortlessly as your
body yields its scent.

~ *Rumi* [3]

IT'S ALL ABOUT
LOVE

My name is Juliette. I am called by Source to write this book, just as you have been called to read it. After all, you have it in your hand. Can we agree that the flow of the Universe has brought us together? I mean... seriously! *You* are reading *my book!* Thank you Divine Spirit...Let the *magic* begin!

This book is about change, evolution, growth and courage on your LifesPath™. It's a story about my own personal roller coaster, and how I have learned to walk on my LifesPath™, in order to draft the road map for you to walk on yours.

SAY YES!

2

This book is about flow, vibration, honesty, and waking up. My hope is that you experience the Four Tenets of Love. You can be a different person when you can look in the mirror and love yourself.

Before you start, I have a favor to ask. Say *yes* and breathe deeply. Say *yes* to opening up your mind and heart. Say *yes* to doing the work and the practice so that your LifesPath™ will take you to magic, truth and love.

Say yes! Now enjoy!

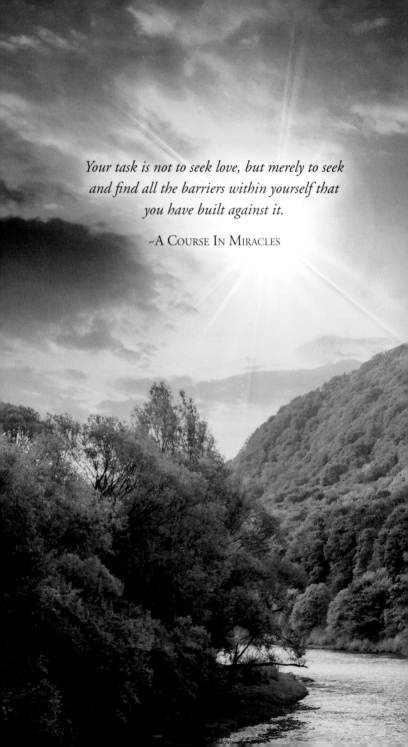

Your task is not to seek love, but merely to seek and find all the barriers within yourself that you have built against it.

~A Course In Miracles

LET IT FLOW

Flow begins with restlessness and a stirring that there is more, that you deserve more, and that there is a better way. Restlessness and stirring is the first step to the Work on your LifesPath™.

You didn't feel this by accident. Your soul is calling out to you and saying, "I am here. I *am*."

If you've lost your flow, you've lost your way.

The Universe and everything within it exists as energy. The energetic flow is the lifeblood of all you see around you and all that you cannot see with your eyes.

All is energy, you are energy, and the flow moves through you and provides all you need on your LifesPath™. The Universe has your back. You are supposed to flow along with the Universe, not against it. When you no longer feel connected to the Universe—when the idea of oneness ceases to resonate—your flow is blocked and your power may be lost.

When did you let your power go? When was it taken away? Think about it.

HOW CAN I CHANGE MY NEGATIVE MINDSET AND REWRITE THIS STORY SO THAT I CAN LIVE A NEW STORY—ONE FILLED WITH PASSION, PURPOSE AND POTENTIAL?

Changing your story is not about reliving the past or festering in trauma. All that does is repeat the same sad song as you keep re-listening...shuffle, repeat, back to that song, shuffle, repeat, back to that song.

When you are in the "flow," your song can and will change. The song can be fresh and exciting. The new song can move you forward into a new story—one that listens to the calling of your soul.

You know deep inside that you want to be a different person, one who is more deeply in touch with love.

HOW CAN I TRANSFORM?

I know it often feels like the hill is slippery with mud and tears. Here is my promise to you.

The answer is always *love*.

ONCE YOU CAN TRULY FEEL LIFE'S FLOW,
LOVE BECOMES A CONSTANT, NOT A GOAL.

You are good enough, bold enough, strong enough, and you can learn to love yourself.

If you only take one thing away from my book, let it be this:

You are only living in *this moment*.
Breathe it in, deeply. Don't regret the past.

The past is what got you here. The past is not real. It doesn't even exist. Your LifesPath™ is ahead of you, not behind you.

Our brain does a very good job of creating recordings of thought patterns that play back the past. This pattern has to be shifted so that new thoughts and energies can become vital. **Once you truly feel life's flow, love becomes a constant, not a goal.**

When you become the moment, the Universe becomes your guide and infinite potential is your currency.

VIBRATION
IS LIFE.

THIS IS LIFE,
GLORIOUS LIFE!

Follow the rhythm of the signs. Place one foot in front of the other and vibrate with the reality of what is and what can be.

We know that energy is all there is and that every thing vibrates. Vibration is life.

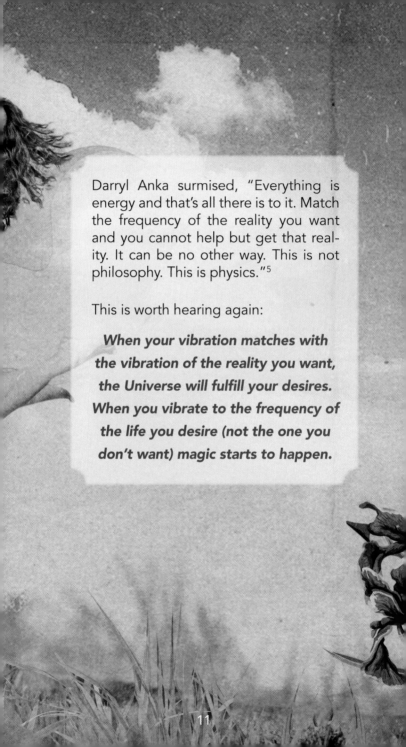

Darryl Anka surmised, "Everything is energy and that's all there is to it. Match the frequency of the reality you want and you cannot help but get that reality. It can be no other way. This is not philosophy. This is physics."[5]

This is worth hearing again:

When your vibration matches with the vibration of the reality you want, the Universe will fulfill your desires. When you vibrate to the frequency of the life you desire (not the one you don't want) magic starts to happen.

OPEN TO MY TRUTH

Decide that you don't want to play that old song. Decide that you don't want to listen to the negative voice holding you back. Decide that you don't want to give up your power.

I have been divorced twice, have been married three times and have been engaged more times than I care to count. My pattern of firebombing and then leaving the relationship became obvious to me after my second divorce. The pattern began to manifest early on in my new relationship. What was the pattern? What was the belief system trying to prove itself true?

When I was two, my family lived in Holland. My parents would occasionally leave me alone in the apartment and go to the apartment downstairs to visit with friends. They thought I was asleep. When they would come back, they would think I was still sleeping. But I would wake up and go into their bedroom thinking they were there and then run back and jump under my covers, scared and worried. I would hear them come home and when they came to check on me, I would pretend to be asleep.

I believed that I would always be alone and even though I may think that people are there for me, they aren't anywhere to be found. I repeated that pattern of pretending to be asleep, pretending I didn't notice things and pretending that all was well and people *were* there for me. My pattern was to prove this story true over and over again. This moment was my root event, not the traumas that I experienced and relived on the therapist couch. No, this event was buried so deep that I hadn't even remembered it as I was reliving my childhood.

Whoa Baby! I know my pattern. I know that I will pretend all is well and be suspicious that all is not well. I know that I am alone and that the life I am in with this person is a fraud, fake, an illusion. So when I can't take it anymore, I take off and before I take off, I firebomb the relationship so that I will be alone. And since I don't really want to be alone, I start all over with a new relationship.

We create the pattern of our core event the moment we realize we are on our own and can't let the world show our true light and brilliance. This pattern is re-created over and over again, with various people, in various places, at various times. It is re-created even when we know that this pattern is harmful and not for our greatest and highest good.

It was time to go deep before I screwed up another marriage. I realized that I needed to truly transform my relationship with the Universe. My marriage—and my life— were giving clear messages that my flow needed some serious maintenance.

Performing maintenance on my life requires a practice and the practice is the Work. Doing the Work can be painful at times and it never stops. But, the Work is rewarding and can be life changing because you become who you were always meant to be, and you can never go back because now you *know*.

THE
LESSON

LET LOVE FLOW

Love is the language of transformation, the answer to life's ills, and the key energy flow of an honest belief system bringing abundance.

In order to have the life you know you can have, and to bring you into the Universal flow, you have to create a new belief system.

The belief system that you have now, that you may not even be aware of, is the one you inherited from your parents, the one you learned when you were young, the one you used to "fit in" and stay connected to your family. These belief systems are ingrained in you so deeply, they are at play without you even being aware of it. They are the foundation of what's stopping you—what's holding you back from breaking through to your most glorious life.

You deserve a glorious life. Experiencing abundance doesn't take anything away from someone else. *It's not a limited resource.* It is unlimited, bountiful, and renewable. I *know*— because I am *living* that glorious life.

The key to creating a new belief system is to fully and honestly understand your old belief system. You have to see the patterns in your life and then say, "What in this pattern is serving me?"

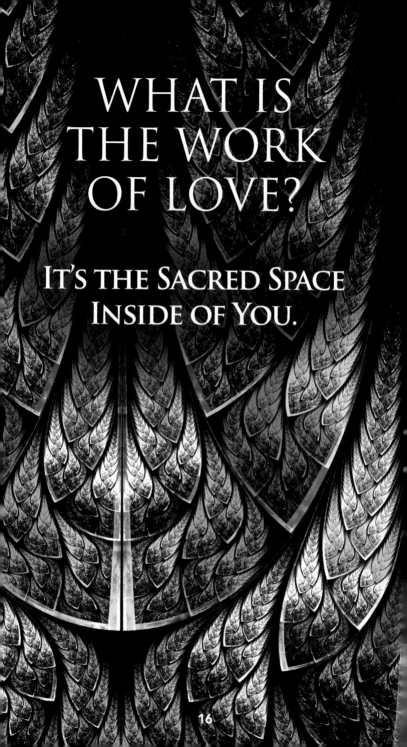

WHAT IS THE WORK OF LOVE?

IT'S THE SACRED SPACE INSIDE OF YOU.

The Work has been, and continues to be, a blessing. The Work is the space between breaths. The Work is nature and sacred space. The Work is the whisper, the call, the nudge, and the push within the moment to shake off fears. It allows the "aha" moment to show up.

The Work is where fear is lost and love is found. The Work is the Universe having the most intimate conversation with you. The Work is where you find the answers. With the Work woven into your LifesPath™, you create a future that manifests abundance and serves your higher purpose.

What is the Work?

The Work is taking the time to nourish your physical body, intellectual mind, emotions, and your soul.

YOU do the Work.

There is no teacher, no method, no guru.[6] The Divine in *you* is the highest voice. Getting to the point where you can hear and not doubt, and then trust and experience it in your body...this is the Work.

What is the Work?

The Work unlocks *you*—your soul. The Work unblocks fear—your separateness from *you*. The Work unleashes your purpose and mission. The Work uncovers your intuition. The Work knows what you want and tells the Universe. The Work manifests your destiny and creates your future.

The Work is taking a leap of faith into the unknown and propelling yourself into your life— the life you want, the life you know you can have, the life you were meant to live *now*, and the life you were meant to love.

Ask yourself, "So what's my story?"

What is the belief system that keeps stopping you? Every time you get close to getting what you want and deserve, you create a situation that allows your old belief system to play out.

While you may not be happy when it plays out, the old belief system wants to prove itself right.

You stay in *paradigm paralysis* instead of moving into a *paradigm shift*.

Moving into a new space requires you to step into the unknown for a moment or two. You may have to stand on shaky ground in order to plant yourself on terra firma.

When you see your old belief system, do the opposite of what you would normally do. Look at the situation as an observer, seeing yourself outside the situation. The original experience is the trigger for your old belief system to show up and cloud your perception of the current situation.

THE WORK
MEANS STEPPING
INTO THE
UNKNOWN.

UNIVERSAL LAWS

Evolution

ev·o·lu·tion [ev-uh-loo-shuhn or, esp. British, ee-vuh-]

Any process of formation or growth; development.[8]

The Work is all about evolution. As you look through this book, every lesson—every word— is a light for you to follow on your LifesPath™. Evolution is a process, a journey of changing your mind, finding your essence, and opening your heart.

Expanding your awareness is a constant practice and truly the heart of the Work. When you are "Letting it flow" and your heart is "Open to possibility," you become aware of infinite potential all around you. To become fully aware, I find it helps to understand the "rules." These are the Laws of the Universe.

The application of all of the Laws is another book. For now, focus on these seven ways of expanding your awareness and using the Work to create magic in your life.

22

Law of Cause and Effect—Nothing happens by chance or outside the Universal Laws. Every thing you do creates a vibration (including thought) and there is a reaction or consequence. Every thought, word or action sets off a wave of energy. Your highest vibration will come back to you after it travels through the Universe. Prosperity is created by our deeds and thoughts.

Law of Divine Oneness—Everything within the Universe is connected to everything else. We are all untapped and unlimited potential. We are always connected to the Universe and the energy of Source. If you believe that you are constantly connected to the Universe, the purest love, then the Universe will clear your path and flow with you.

Law of Attraction—This ubiquitous concept is a critical element of using the Laws to bring abundance into your life. It is best understood in its simplest terms: positive energy attracts positive energy, negative energy attracts negative energy.

The Law of Attraction is not only about "thinking" positively, though thoughts are an *important* part of creating the high vibration that you want to be your language. It's also about taking positive *action*.

Law of Action—The Universe will bring you infinite opportunities. Being in the right vibration is essential to attracting the opportunities you desire. By applying the Law of Action, you can be an effective creator, and that starts with setting clear intentions, and committing to a plan. You can have anything you desire, but you must engage in actions that support your thoughts and dreams, emotions, and words.

Law of Polarity—This is the law of mental vibrations. We can suppress and transform undesirable thoughts by concentrating on the opposite pole. For example, if you carry a prejudice or judgment in your vibration, your auric field will transmit that negative energy into the Universe. However, you can turn that dark expression into light by focusing on the opposite of judgment, *unconditional love.*

Remember that people, events and circumstances all just exist. It's how you *perceive* them that makes them good or bad. You are the creator. It's your choice whether you smile or frown. It's entirely up to you whether you experience joy or sadness. You have the power to choose either end of the spectrum.

Law of Vibration—Everything in the Universe vibrates. Each sound, object, and even thoughts have their own vibrational frequency.

The Law of Perpetual Transmutation of Energy—The energy of the Universe is moving, constantly. Change is all there is.

CHANGE IS THE ONLY CONSTANT.

LET'S
MEDITATE

Meditation can take on many different forms. I know people who can meditate on the subway, and others must have their sacred space meticulously prepared—pillow, candles, incense and the perfect music. If you have a practice that works for you, great! If you are just starting out, get comfortable, close your eyes and go!

For the meditations, I am asking you to clear your schedule and create the space that will best inspire you and give you a feeling of safety. This meditation is all about *flow!*

Stand with bare feet, outside if possible, so you can be completely grounded in the earth. Inside works, too, but use every opportunity you get to meditate outside. Take some deep cleansing breaths. REALLY breathe. Breath in through your nostrils and out through your mouth. Place your hands by your side and stand solid like a tree. Imagine that your toes and the soles of your feet are moving through the earth—down, down, down to the center of the earth. Allow yourself to visualize your toes hooking onto a bar or a ring. Stand on terra firma. Breathe deep cleansing breaths. Feel the energy moving down to the center. Then feel the energy moving up through your legs and into your core.

Lift your arms up to the sky, stretching your fingers out as far as you can and look up. Imagine this earth energy you have brought into you moves out through your arms up and into the sky as high as you can.

Now take a few cleansing breaths and feel the energy of the sky enter your fingers, then down your arms and then into the top of your head. Move it down to your core and then down into the earth. This creates a constant loop of energy moving from the earth into you and through the Universe.

Wonderful right? Visualizing and then using your personal energy system is one of the most important points in your evolution.

AFFIRMATION

I am in complete flow, and all that needs to move, moves freely through me. My energy is recharged as it moves through me. I am alive. I let fear go and I let love flow.

OPEN UP YOUR HEART TO INFINITE POSSIBILITIES

"The most beautiful things in the world cannot be seen or even touched, they must be felt with the heart."⁹

~HELEN KELLER

In Tenet One, I shared my feelings about flow and energy, and the deep work of breaking patterns, and letting life unfold with you as creator. These ideas about visualization and vibration may seem odd, but please trust me. This stuff is AH-mazing and life-changing.

Once you fully understand and believe in vibration —with your heart and soul, not just your brain—and its critical influence on you, the world truly opens up into unlimited potential to explore!

Tenet Two is all about opening your heart to the infinite possibilities. Opening your heart is essential to your evolution.

Look beyond what is real *now* and visualize what *can be*. When love is your language, and your heart is fully generating its wonderful vibration, you can consciously create the future you desire.

We must have a deep love affair with *ourselves*. We need to learn to love and cherish all parts of ourselves.

FIRST, CHANGE YOUR MIND ABOUT YOU!

Loving yourself is about opening up your heart to receive. Until you can fully love yourself, you will continue to live at the lowest frequency of fear rather than the highest frequency of love.

LET LOVE BE YOUR

Your heart is sometimes like a flower in the dark, closing up, and when the light shines on your heart, opening fully. Your open heart leans towards the light, ready for all possibilities and opportunities to unfold. Your heart opens to synchronicity and coincidences, knowing they are meant for you, and knowing all will come your way.

We are not meant to swim upstream against the life force, we are meant to flow downstream, *with* the life force. In this case, the Work is swimming with the current and each time gaining a little more traction. This is something you have to do consciously. By assimilating the new experiences and energy charge, it changes you and brings about an awareness of the underlying current.

FIRST LANGUAGE.

This continual assimilation brings about new events that you think occur by chance, but aren't by chance. These events guide us forward and then bring us more awareness of ourselves and the notion that we have a purpose and a destiny. Once this happens, the energy that actualized the events stays with us and we increase our vibration, opening up to even more awareness, and more "chance occurrences."

Evolution to a higher vibration.

So what stops us? We know our own belief system stops the flow of energy, and with the Work, we can rebuild a belief system that suits us. Now, if you can open your heart, and let love be your first language, your vibration will soon lead you to a more evolved LifesPath™ and a world of infinite possibilities.

There are 37.2 trillion cells in your body constantly changing at a pace faster than you can imagine. The cells that make up your body now are not the same cells that you will go to bed with tonight. These cells are constantly adjusting and reshuffling as they process information, keep your heart beating, and keep your lungs breathing.

Most of this information will be influenced and redefined based on your mind—but it is your heart that is the center of love, and the generator of your energy system.

This love I'm talking about is a love that is so pure and divine, we need do nothing but surrender ourselves to it.

This love is one that is completely open and requires our complete trust that it can take our pain, hurt, anger, and hatred away—but we must claim it, own it, give it away to love, and then surrender to it completely.

Watch out for those sneaky old BELIEF SYSTEMS!

They're sneaky little bastards...and they keep coming back because we keep believing them.

All of these beliefs boil down to "I don't deserve...," or "It can't be so easy to..." In their most elemental layer it's the belief that you don't deserve love or to be loved. You believe you don't deserve the gifts the Universe is giving you, so you stop the movie, you stop the play, you stop, and you rewind, and play it again up to that same place, and then you stop. Again.

OPEN TO MY TRUTH

Love yourself so much that you can't do anything that doesn't make you love yourself more.

I love my bed...the smell, the heaviness of the down comforter, and the softness of the pillows. I leave one foot out in the cold, because I enjoy having the window open while my body is cuddled deep in the folds of the comforter.

Usually before going to sleep, I read for a minute or two and then I start to drift into that space between the dream and awake world.

As I drift into this space, I remember the owl who greeted me and showed me a vision of an event in the future. I remember the following day that he swept down and dragged off a chipmunk while my daughter Dagen and I were waiting for her bus. Then the hawk who had circled above me for days—screeching and circling, screeching and circling...

While we sleep, we can travel in the other realms of consciousness with relative ease.

Caroline Myss states that, "I believe that to be a 'mystic without a monestary' is a new 'soul's calling'..."[11] I've been thinking about that a lot. To me, being a mystic without a monastery implies that mystics are without the structures, the histories and the support of a system. They do not need nor desire to follow the traditions and protocols, so they do their Work outside of the hierarchies set in place.

As a modern mystic I enjoy companionship, friendships, and sisterhood. I am not a follower, and am not interested in rebuilding a structure in the New Age like the structures before.

The Work is a solo job. This is work where the initiation takes place in dreamworld, in the inner travels of my soul as we commune and become one with the divine.

I am a mystic without a monastery.

And I'm ok. You will be, too.

THE
LESSON

OPEN YOUR HEART TO THE FULL POTENTIAL OF YOUR SOUL'S PURPOSE.

To start living at the highest frequency of love instead of the lowest frequency of fear, you must open your heart and soul to potential! Here are some steps for Opening to Possibilities:

Take time for yourself. Find sacred space. Dream and daydream about what is possible, about where you want to be, about how you want it to look.

Spend time in nature. When your mind is quiet, the vibration of Mother Earth brings balance and connection to your energy. Let the soft breeze and scudding clouds embrace you while Spirit inspires imagination. Who do you want to be?

Every breath is filled with possibility. Isn't life supposed to be an adventure? The leaves rustling in the background are the noise of peacefulness, the tranquility of time stopping completely. Listen inside of you, close your eyes, and let the breeze cleanse you. Feel deep into your soul. Where do you actually feel it in your body?

Our heart knows the path to happiness and inner peace. Consistent practice of meditation and prayer remind us of what we already know.

When we forget our heart's message and fall into life's ruts and crevices, we feel unfulfilled and unhappy. We get depressed and anxious. We have blurred our perspective, forgotten the bigger picture, and lost our way.

The remedy is simple. Take the time to remember your divinity, your spiritual nature. Remember why you are here.

CHAKRAS

This lesson is all about *Chakras*—centers in your body where energy flows through. Blocks in your *Chakras* can cause everything from illness to difficulties in living a happy life. I will show you how to activate your *Chakras* and use their power to open your heart and galvanize your energy. When you do this, you are empowered as the creator of your own life!

I am going to make this ancient and complex concept easy to understand and use, so you can create abundance and flow in your life. My message to you is this:

Don't question. Believe.

Here is a simple way to visualize your interaction with the world around you. Use your imagination freely to envision your connection to Source and the divine energetic system within your body.

Close your eyes, and focus in on identifying your main *Chakras,* starting at the red root—the foundation of who you are in this world. Work your way up, one by one, all the way to your crown *Chakra,* the connecting point to the All-That-Is.

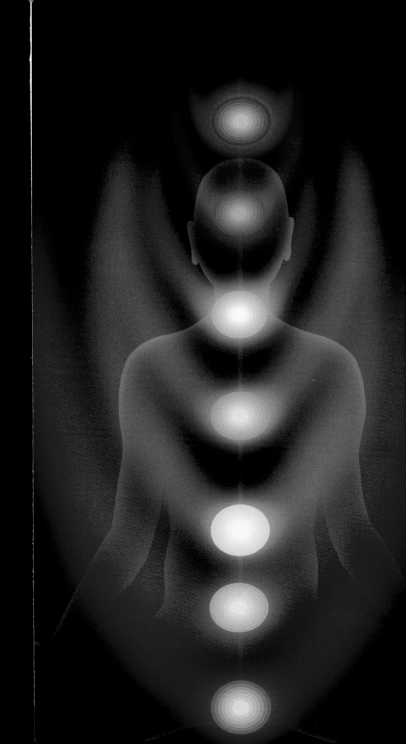

Chakra is the ancient Indian Sanskrit word for wheel. It defines the seven main energy centers in the human body. Each wheel draws energy to the physical, mental, emotional, and spiritual body.

These colorful centers are connected by even smaller centers called meridians throughout your body and are tied directly to your continual connection to the Universe.

Your internal energy wiring system is your *Chakra* system. You are both a transmitter and receiver of energy and vibration.

Visualize your body as if you were an electronic device, with lights and sounds. Your very thoughts and emotions carry a vibrational "charge" from within your "perceived" body to your auric field. The auric field is the direct interface between you, your environment, people around you, and the whole entire Universe.

If you can believe that electricity and radio waves—all vibrations—can transmit messages, then you can believe this, as well. We are all energy. By practicing these visualizations and using them in your meditation ritual, you will become expert in recharging your energy, and creating flow through your *Chakra* system.

You will move closer to the ideal of a constant interchange between you and your world, and allow for the free flow of love, trust in the Universe, and gratitude. This will expand the opportunities and the magic in your life.

Following is a classic *Chakra* illustration, with very brief explanations of what each *Chakra* can mean to your evolution.

In my experience, the lower *Chakras* are where our biggest issues and blockages lie, and must be cleared regularly to support an open heart, and the highest vibration.

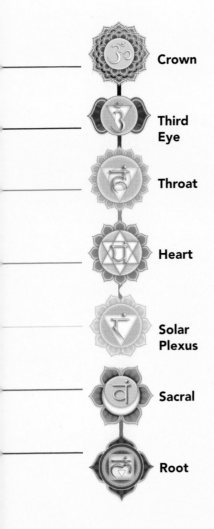

Crown

Third
Eye

Throat

Heart

Solar
Plexus

Sacral

Root

These *Chakra* areas
show how and where we
connect energetically
to the earth, the world,
to other people, and to
Divine Light.

Root: This is the seat of your sense of security and survival. It is critical that you solidify your *Muladhara* and build a confident core to support you in the world. This *Chakra* is effected by financial and career upheaval, and can really impede spiritual growth if it is ignored. This area is deeply tied to self-image, and our perceived role as provider for ourselves, and our dependents. Healthy food and sleep are essential to building this foundation.

Sacral: This orange center called *Swadhisthana* is where your real power lies. Sexual energy and the spark of creativity live here, as well as the verve needed to make life full and rich. This is the center of pleasure, desire and reproductive energy. Your inner child lives and plays here.

Solar Plexus: Remember the classic line of "fire in the belly" to describe real fiery enthusiasm? Right below your ribcage and in the center of both fear and your self-image, *Manipura* is an ego center, and the main obstacle to self-love. Before you can really embrace yourself with honesty, you must deal with this yellow energy, and face yourself in the mirror, forgiving, loving and strengthening your inner power. It is also the center of how you bring your mission, purpose, and your Work into the world—so it's no surprise that when you exercise, the most important part is to work your core!

Heart: *Anahata* is the center of love and compassion. When your heart is open, everything is easier in life. When your lower *Chakras* are freed, and the Kundalini energy swirls into your heart space, you will feel joy and connection. This is where the highest vibration begins to form, creating the language of unconditional love and highest potential—fueling creativity with passion! It is also where all healing takes place, since we get dis-eased from the outside in and we heal from the inside out.

Throat: If you can't find your voice, chances are it is blocked at *Vishuddhi*. Sometimes this manifests as a "lump" in your throat (something deeply personal that needs to be shared) or a deep frustration at not "being heard." This *Chakra* acts like a filter, and can become a censor if you are unsure about your words and expression. When this turquoise blue center is free and energized, your truth flows freely, and your highest vibration is shared. It is where your authentic voice and action reside—without the voice to bring the "Word to Flesh," you cannot create the visions you manifest.

Third Eye: The Third Eye, or *Ajna*, is the point of connection between you and your spiritual portal, the pineal gland. In addition to producing the sleep hormone melatonin, this light-sensitive gland produces DMT, the bodies own hallucinogen—a powerful and transformative substance that may be the secret to the connection between humans and the Divine. *Ajna* brings connection to other dimensions, where guides and spiritual beings reside.

Crown: *Sahasrara* means thousand-petaled Lotus, and a state of pure consciousness can be obtained when the flower fully opens. During deep meditation, wisdom and visions of universal unity are common, as well as direct communication with Source. It takes real commitment to reach the utterly ecstatic moment of greater consciousness. It is worth it!

LET'S
MEDITATE

Sit in a comfortable position on the floor or in a chair. Take several deep breaths, centering yourself, and focusing on your breath. Calm each part of your body starting with your head and shoulders and ending with your toes. As you relax, think about your heart being surrounded by a pink bubble. Visualize the iridescence of the bubble, and how it floats.

Now imagine the beautiful, airy, pink bubble growing. Imagine you are completely wrapped inside the bubble. As it continues to grow bigger and bigger, your room is now inside the bubble. Feel the walls nestled inside it. Now the bubble is engulfing your home in its soft grasp, as it expands around your neighborhood. You rise into the air, above everything, and watch how your town is in the bubble now, all the towns around you, now your state, your country, the continent, and then the whole world.

Visualize yourself floating in space, but close by the beautiful blue earth, in deep silence, floating effortlessly. Now watch the earth become engulfed by the pink, glowing bubble, full of everyone you love and everything that makes you smile.

Feel all of this wrapped inside of the bubble, and slowly reach forward and cup the soft pinkness in the palm of your hand. You are holding the sacred container of all life!

Now place that bubble into your heart. It will softly disappear into your chest. Feel the warmth moving through you, out to your toes and fingers, deep into your stomach and heart.

AFFIRMATION

I open my heart with abandon and grace. I am a vehicle for the Universe to shower me with love. I am love, I am loved, I love. I embrace and accept all the love there is to give and I give love back with an open heart.

"We are a reflection of ourselves manifested in the Universe and reflected back to us."

~MARCUS AURELIUS

VIEW THE WORLD AS A BLANK CANVAS— YOURS TO FILL!

We know a few amazing things:

- The Universe vibrates.
- All living things have energy fields.
- We have an energy field around us that connects us to everything in the Universe.
- Things shift and morph based on the observation of the observer (what the observer wants).
- Plants, trees and animals have a symbiotic relationship with us. We share breath, light and energy.

When we elevate our vibrations, we create an atmosphere of love and well-being, and we resonate with the Universe. It wants to vibrate at a higher frequency—happy and high vs. sad and low.

Particle Physicist Don Lincoln said "Quantum fields are really a mind-bending way of thinking. Everything—and I mean everything—is just a consequence of many infinitely-large fields vibrating. The entire Universe is made of fields playing a vast, subatomic symphony. Physicists are trying to understand the melody."[12]

There are times that clients are unwilling to learn the details of vibration and *Chakras*, one stating quite clearly that she thought "coaching" had nothing to do with science. The more you understand the "Flow" of energy within your body and your connection to the Universe, the faster you can bring *magic* into your life.

One important element to remember is that *imagination* and *believing* are key to energy work. Make it part of your practice to read about *Chakra* energy. Look at how artists and scientists depict and describe the elements of your system. Take a few Kundalini Yoga classes as a way to awaken your perceptions and energize your flow.

The deeper your mastery of *Chakras*, the easier it becomes to identify and break blockages, where those Gremlins may be hanging out.

Please, give yourself permission to believe in magic! Quantum Theory will explain everything in scientific terms eventually.

Until then, believe...

"Out of the blue I felt it, the feeling of nothingness. 'Who am I?' was the question and out of the blue, the answer came. I am nothing and with that I realized I am everything.

I am the leaf on the tree that sways in the wind. I am the butterfly that flitters gracefully from one flower to the next. I am the dogs barking at night. I am the waves crashing against the rocks in the Pacific and I am the soft swells that reach the shore of the Atlantic. I am everything and I am nothing—but a part of everything. I am connected to the All That Is and it is in me."

~Juliette Taylor-De Vries

WHO AM I?

LIVE BIG AND BRIGHTLY!

One of the things I think is so very important is to know that you are supposed to dare
to play it *big*. What good are your talents
and dreams if they stay in your mind? If you
don't believe it can happen for you, it won't.
It's your canvas! Paint it bright, beautiful, and
exactly the way you want it to look.

Clearing your energetic blockages and raising
your vibration will allow the Universe to bring

you every opportunity you can imagine. You decide. You think it. You believe it. It happens.

People need you! They need your work, your passion, your skills, and your talents. Don't waste it by being afraid to jump into it. For years, I was too afraid to actually take the leap of faith and jump in. It's like walking on hot coals. Your mind is saying, "No way is this possible." And yet, that is exactly what it is—possible and actually probable. Just ask Tony Robbins.

Fear is what is holding you back. Fear is a guidepost to change. Without fear, there is no change and no forward movement. Change your focus. Change the way you look at things. Once you change your perception, you change your life, which really does change the world.

Change your thoughts, words, and perceptions and you'll change your story. Change your story and you'll change your life. Change your life and you'll change the world. It all starts with thoughts. Your thoughts create the world you live in as each word and thought vibrates and each vibration alters the world.

When you are ready to change—when you have learned that the unknown and the future are nothing but the Universal Flow of infinite opportunity—you can start to view the world as your mirror.

What do you see when you look out from within your fortress? Remember, perception is everything.

It's about experiencing and relating to the world as the mirror. This is how we find the patterns that keep us in the groove of our old belief systems. It's seeing what you need to see and seeing what is, not what you "think" you see, for your mind moves only in perception and perception is a sliver of reality.

It's what you perceive to be your past. It's a trigger of a collection of experiences, memories, fears, dramas, and hopes that transfer the image and create a perception that you read as truth.

Viewing the world as your mirror is about seeing what you need to see, then reflecting on it and deciding how to respond.

What is inside of you in your mind—your perception—becomes what you see outside of you. It colors your reality in every way.

"Make no mistake about it. Enlightenment is a destructive process. It has nothing to do with becoming better or being happier. Enlightenment is the crumbling away of untruth. It's seeing through the facade of pretense. It's the complete eradication of everything we imagined to be true." [13]

~ADYASHANTI

Dee Wallace (you may remember her as the mom in the movie *E.T.*) affirms the universal truth of conscious creation:

"I am the creation of me. I create me first and my Universe is created. I am the creation of my 'I am' presence."[14]

Who do you see in the mirror?

Do you see your holiness—the true essence of who you are? This is the divine part of us.

Do you see your ego—the false 'me'? Is this the voice that tells you how little you are, how gross, how fat, how skinny, how pathetic?

IT ISN'T REAL. IT'S THE FALSE YOU. Yes, I am yelling it to the world so *all* can hear. It's the *voice* you hear, so it isn't *you*.

Who is this decision maker that chooses whether to listen to that part of the mind that judges and belittles...or celebrates your divine place in a miraculous world?

What immense power makes the decision about whether you smile at yourself in the mirror, and choose love, or frown while you feel fear, guilt and judgment?

You know the answer by now, don't you?

The *you* that *hears* the voice is the decision maker.

Dealing with major stress opens doors for incredible transformation, as it did for me—but you have to be able to see it. I realized, in one fell swoop, how incredibly fragile and short life really can be. In an instant, I realized that it is vital to cling onto every ounce of positive energy you encounter in order to create the future that you want.

I had been taught that I could overcome any obstacle if I put my mind to it. All the women in my life fostered the notion that I could be anything, I could handle anything, and that I had to be strong—always. (And, of course, have my passport on my person at all times!) But somewhere along the way I lost my voice. I became fearful of the future. I clung onto the storybook plan I had made in my head with a fierceness that was like a torrent of rain. Even though it was washing more and more of my Spirit into a place further and further away from me, I still clung onto it.

It was like walking upstream. I don't know how salmon do it, but I know one thing: we are not meant to force our way upstream. We are not meant to fight against the waves. We are meant to dive in and let the waves carry us to that stillness of the shoreline, where the ebb and flow can be felt with a softness of a kiss from your child—not with the ferocity of a slap in the face.

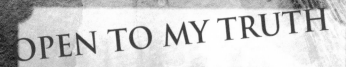

OPEN TO MY TRUTH

Step into the moment even if it is so scary and you are frozen with fear. With suffering comes awakening.

When he came back from his third combat tour, one to Afghanistan and two to Iraq, something was different. We lived with the "nothing is the matter with me" phantom for months.

Then one morning I was banging on the door of his office and I had the worst feeling of what I would see on the other side. My voice said, "Don't go in there, don't do it. *Run, run, run!*" Instead I found a hairpin and unlocked the door to find him holding a pistol and pointing at me and then pointing at himself. Now you would think this was my rock bottom, my dark night of the soul. No. This was the beginning of the descent to my Hell on Earth.

As I stood there, staring into the barrel of his gun, I told myself, "This is not happening. This is not the fairy tale I signed up for." His eyes were locked on me as if I was a target.

His hands shaking slightly, he whispered, "I'm not sure whether I should shoot you..." Then he turned the gun toward himself and muttered, "Or myself."

Have you had a moment where something so horrible is happening that it feels impossible for the event to be really occurring? It's during those surreal moments that we have to rely strongly on our inner strength, fortitude, stamina, and take a breath.

"Breathe, Juliette, just breathe" became my mantra at that moment. All else went blank. In fact, I actually couldn't see. Everything was a blur and his voice was coming from far, far away. I stood there, trying to focus on the man I loved while my brain tried to figure out how to escape, how to disappear, to rewind to the first moment when I knew something wasn't right.

I was frozen in this moment of time. I was trapped in a nightmare—one that was never going to end.

THE
LESSON

YOUR OLD STORY IS NOT YOU. YOU CAN
BEGIN LOVING YOURSELF AND START
TODAY WITH A BLANK CANVAS THAT IS
YOURS TO FILL WITH NEW STORIES FILLED
WITH LOVE.

Here are some steps you can take to begin viewing the world as a blank canvas that you get to fill in:

Explore your story: *Who are you?* This is the first step to finding out who you are and what you are meant to do. *Who are you really? Who do you dream of being and of doing?* The doing is the soul's purpose—your soul's purpose and destiny. Don't regret the past or fear the future. Live in that Holy Instant—the place where you just are. The "I *am* moment." I am...(those words that follow will change your world.)

Focus on what's good in your life and ask for more of it. We spend a lot of energy focusing on what's wrong with our lives or what's lacking. This only gives us more of the same, since the Universe only understands how to give you more of what you ask for.

Adapt to your flow. Create a routine that includes *me* time. We all say we don't have time. We do have time! We check our messages, we text, we Facebook message, we tweet, we worry. Why can't we spend time on us? Just an hour per day has the power to manifest a new you—the one you dream of being, the one you know you are.

Start mindful and purposeful thinking. Think about the actual words you are using. Words carry energetic vibrations and affect the cells in your body, and your perception of the world around you.

"When you say, 'I have a sad heart,' then you literally have a sad heart. If we looked inside your heart, we would find it affected by molecules that cause stress and damage, such as excessive amounts of adrenaline and cortisol. If you say, 'I'm busting with joy,' a scientist could analyze your skin and find it loaded with neuropeptides that may have antidepressant effects and that may modulate the immune system. If you say, 'I feel exhilarated, unbounded and joyful,' a doctor examining your blood would find high levels of interleuken and interferon, both powerful anticancer drugs. Can you imagine how powerful that is?" [15]

~Deepak Chopra

Life is supposed to be easy—not hard.
Life is supposed to flow.
Life is supposed to be filled with infinite possibilities.

What does it look like when life is easy and flowing? Focus in on yourself in this moment. What are you wearing? What smells and sights are around you? Experience in your body what it's like being in this place. Sit with it. Daydream about it. Pretend you are already there.

To get to the feeling where your life flows and is filled with infinite possibilities, you have to be able to imagine what it looks like. One way to get used to feeling comfortable with daydreaming is to take a few minutes every day at the same time and visualize what you want. Rather than focusing on your goals, such as, "I want a new car," focus on the *feeling* behind the desire. Say to yourself, "I want to feel...excited, loved, accepted." *(You fill in the blank.)*

Once you know what it is that you want, go to a mirror and say to yourself out loud, "I am...*(You fill in the blank.)*

It may feel funny at first, or it may bring up a lot of emotions—and not all of them pleasant. Go with it. Keep saying it every morning and every night before you go to bed.

Sooner than you think, you may not feel so funny, weird, or ridiculous. You will begin to see the love in your own eyes—for yourself. This is what you look like when you are filled with self-love. This is being centered on Self and is much different than being self-centered.

Self-centered is fear-based and means you don't think you are good enough—so you're going to try to prove to the world that you *are* enough.

Being centered on self means that you love yourself for who you are right now. You accept yourself for where you are in the moment and you stand tall in your authenticity. You are the real you, all the time, in all ways, and always.

What does it look like when you are centered on Self?

This is the Work—creating your life with passion and purpose, and realizing the infinite opportunities all around. Start by daydreaming about what it would look like if you were completely and fully centered on loving yourself—as your own best friend. Love yourself beyond anyone or anything else.

The most fundamental message is to love the self. Not the ego, but the 'you' that listens to the nasty dissatisfied voice that tells you all the things that are wrong with you, all the ways you made the wrong choices, and all the moments you took a misstep.

The self is the real you, the 'you' that is directly linked to the Divine. The ego is the fake you, the boxed-up you, the one that tells you either that you are not good enough or that you are so much better than everyone else. It's not telling you that you are *one* with everyone and everything else, that you are not alone, that you are connected to the *All-That-Is*. This nasty voice is the gremlin inside your head—and nothing quiets that voice like love.

Instead of listening to it and then arguing with it, start treating it like the crazy aunt that babbles and jammers about everything and nothing, and always with a pinch of negativity. Let it ramble and then appease it by saying, "Sure you may have a point...and I'll try this other way anyway."

LET'S
MEDITATE

Try to do this in the evening in a place that is quiet and feels secure and snuggly.

Close your eyes and try to think, feel and re-experience something that gave you pleasure today. It can be as simple as a kiss from your child or a smile from a store clerk. (The point is to train your body and mind to register these things during the day in preparation for this evening meditation ritual.) Where are you feeling this in your body? What does it look like, feel like, smell like, and sound like? Savor this re-lived moment. Try to activate all five senses.

This practice will train you to notice all the beautiful things unfolding in your life on a daily basis. It allows you to express the sensation of gratitude for what you have right here, right now—not in a day, a year or five years from now. You'll begin to see the beauty in the smallest of things: the rain falling onto a puddle, the smile of a stranger, the sunlight peaking through the clouds, the birds chirping. The more you meditate, the more you will notice what is beautiful around you, and thus raise your vibration.

"Meditation" can be done any-where, and what I am describing can be just as powerful whether you are waiting in line at the grocery store or sitting in the traditional lotus position.

The key to meditation success is to create energetic flow.

The following meditation focuses on your senses first instead of your *Chakras*.

AFFIRMATION

I am in the exact right place at the exact right time and I am grateful to the Universe.

As you sit, hold your hands over your heart. Now you are letting love infuse your being. Love is your essence... your language. Visualize your heart expanding with beautiful, lush, green energy. Feel the love course through your body, touching your memories, and highlighting the moments of openness and flow of your day.

To fully realize the power of love as the language of evolution and transformation, start your day in the same space as you ended the night before.

Find the moment between wakefulness and sleep, and stay there for a few minutes, focusing only on the expression of love. Fill yourself with this energy, and then open your eyes to greet the day with joy and anticipation.

"*The key to growth is the introduction
of higher dimensions of consciousness into
our awareness.*"

~Lao Tzu

TENET FOUR

EXPAND YOUR AWARENESS

MOVE YOUR ENERGY FROM ANGER TO LOVE.

All beings have within them the power to change the conditions of their lives. Higher vibrations consume and transform lower ones, allowing each of us to change the energies in our lives at any point.

Remember that love is the language with the highest vibration.

An Exercise in Evolution
The purpose of this exercise is to tap into a low vibration—and shift it, so try to do this when you are feeling good.

Start your day with a heart-opening meditation—any featured in this book will work. Your goal is to go to a very public place, and interact with a wide range of people. Your local grocery store or the shopping mall are both perfect destinations.

While walking around, or sitting in an open spot, look at different people, particularly those who you normally might judge. If obese people bother you, or people of color, or moms with screaming kids...I think you understand. Find a person or situation that "irritates" you or gives you a feeling of anger or even hate.

After you find that low vibration feeling or voice, stop, and focus on your reaction. Where does it come from? What part of your body sense is heightened when you feel anger or irritation?

Usually your feelings of judgment come from your lower Chakras, and are driven by your own low self-esteem, so as you move energy from anger to love, your heart Chakra will open and you can create positivity.

The trick is to look at the person and actively turn anger to love—shift any negative feelings to the highest vibration. Every time you identify a negative thought, and shift it to positive, you are literally changing the vibration of your life.

This process needs to occur not just when you go shopping, of course. Every time you make a judgment about a person or situation, you are altering the flow of Universal communication—the Universe doesn't judge, you do. So start to actively shift your vibration. You will become happier and more at ease with the world.

By the end of this book, I want you to feel insightful and inspired! It is time to jump into your dream life and know that you are on the ride of your life. I want you to know you are not alone on your LifesPath™, and that you *can* change your story, and change your life. After all, isn't life supposed to be an adventure? How did you get to the point where you stopped dreaming, stopped exploring and just settled into a boring, mundane life?

DIVE IN!

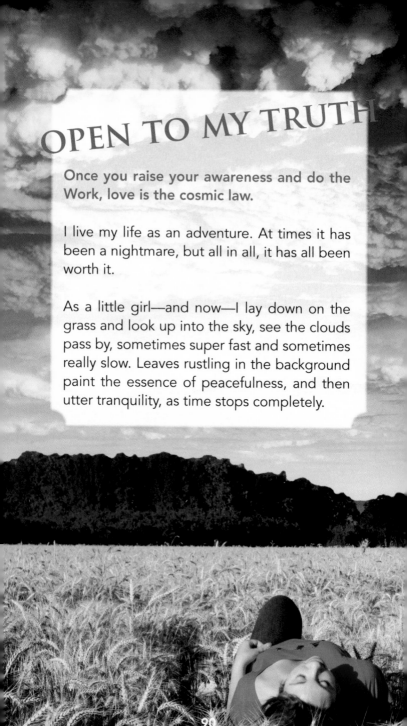

OPEN TO MY TRUTH

Once you raise your awareness and do the Work, love is the cosmic law.

I live my life as an adventure. At times it has been a nightmare, but all in all, it has all been worth it.

As a little girl—and now—I lay down on the grass and look up into the sky, see the clouds pass by, sometimes super fast and sometimes really slow. Leaves rustling in the background paint the essence of peacefulness, and then utter tranquility, as time stops completely.

What is change? Can you acknowledge that life is change? Can you let the light in? Can you live honestly by being the same person you want to be in your dreams? Can you? Yes! Will you? That's up to you. You have a choice. No matter what is happening in your life, you have a choice: To stay and do nothing or break out and take action. There is a recipe for walking on your LifesPath™ with openness, inspiration, and love.

Love is the cosmic law—it's what everything can vibrate to at the highest level. This is manifest creation. When in that state, communication is instantaneous. When the absolute vibrates, it manifests as creation. When love is your language, everything is possible.

LOVE IS THE COSMIC LAW

THE
LESSON

The final lesson centers on the practice, putting the Work to use in creating a life full of wonder, passion, and purpose. The Four Tenets are just a start to begin enjoying the abundance the Universe has to offer you. The Work never stops, it gets deeper, better, and filled with more learnings.

We have focused on rebuilding your belief system by breaking down the patterns blocking you from your abundant life, changing your story by opening your heart, looking at yourself through the eyes of love, so that you can walk on your unique LifesPath™.

One way to vitalize your practice is by understanding and using the **Universal Laws**. Spend some time learning about vibration and the particles of energy that are all around us. There is great power in this work, and it will open the door to meaningful co-creation.

As a modern day shaman, a "shamanista," coach, and creator of the LifesPath™ process, I work with a diverse group of clients who are looking for a deeper and richer life experience with Source. They know they are meant for something more and want to get unstuck. My connection to Source is always on, giving me a gift of insight and often powerful and personal knowledge.

I'm often asked after a reading, "How do you know all of this about me?" I know because your soul tells me through images, songs, riddles, music, symbols, sounds, people who have died, your past lives, and your guides. All of this lives actively in your energy field that I tap into when I prep for the reading. It's all there—the blueprint, the story, the message. It's all in you!

Your soul carries the imprint through the ages and it wants what it wants: to fulfill your cosmic promise of being alive and showing others how to be alive. Follow the cracks in your consciousness and go into the core of you and let go of the rest. Let it bleed out and die.

Leap into the fear of the unknown and then jump for joy that you are on your LifesPath™.

Here are some ways to expand your awareness:

Begin a meditation routine. This powerful practice can energize your *Chakras* if you choose, or allow you to engage your intuition. Your sixth sense taps directly into the Divine Universe, and Spirit guides us during those quiet moments. Start with a few minutes the same time every day and then add more minutes every week. *Meditation is listening, while praying is asking.* Meditation is also a terrific time to manifest.

In *The Secret*, the words *Ask, Believe, Receive* make up the mantra for living your soul's purpose with abundance and for manifesting the life you were/are meant to live. Create your own mantra, and use it during a *Kundalini* energy meditation while you move energy through your *Chakras* and manifest abundance.

ASK,
BELIEVE,
RECEIVE[16]

Breathe deeply and with awareness, and practice the "Healing Art of Loving Touch"[17] as taught by my mentor Meredith Young-Sowers. Cross your arms and place them on your heart and close your eyes. Begin breathing deeply and notice your in breath and your out breath. Feel your heart beating and imagine warmth and light filling your heart up. Feel the Divine Source filling you up with love. Ask to be given love. Ask to be filled with joy.

Now relax and feel what happens next. Sit with it for a moment and then open your eyes. You'll notice that you are more relaxed and feeling like someone just gave you a big hug.

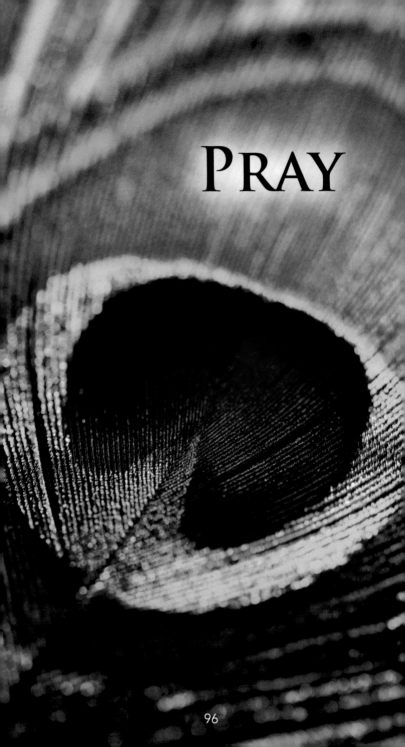

PRAY

Pray: This is where the asking comes in. Before you ask, be grateful, thank God, or Spirit, or whatever you choose to call the Divine Universe for what you already have received and will receive.

Can you make a list of what you are grateful for everyday? I usually do. On the days I don't, I feel like crap and end up focusing on all the wrong things. The Universe gives us more of what we focus on. So don't focus on the bills—focus on the clients, the work you love, and your passions. Visualize your life as spectacular.

Break through your fears of _____ (you fill in the blank):

What are you afraid of? *Clue: It's what keeps you up at night.* Once you know what it is and you acknowledge it, it's not the bogeyman anymore. It's tangible. Hold yourself accountable and own your life without shame or regret.

LET'S
MEDITATE

This exercise is very easy and positive. Find a quiet, comfortable space to sit. On a pad of paper, at the top, write: "I am..." Fill it in with as many positive words as you can. Next, write, "The world is..." and do the same thing. Finally, write, "I love myself and I..." and then write all the positive verbs you can.

Choose three words from your list—the three most powerful to you. These will be your personal Mantra for the meditation. You want to silence any voices that might disturb your inner peace. Instead of listening to yourself, focus on the three words, your mantra. Let's say you chose love, forgive, and potential. Love... forgive... potential...

The following meditation will challenge your powers of visualization.

Put on music that calms you. Sit in lotus position, and breathe three times, through your nose, taking the breath all the way down to your root Chakra. Visualize deep red color at your tail bone, the color and intensity brightening as your solar plexus opens to welcome the breath.

While you breathe steadily, visualize that red luscious glow move from your root up to your sacral area, and repeat your mantra while the color blends and shifts to orange, a glowing bright orange that carries the fire of your sexuality and desire for life's rich opportunity. Let your ego and any judgment drift away, and feel your power. Love... forgive... potential!

You are now activating your solar plexus Chakra. Breathe into your center, right at the base of your rib cage. It is very easy to feel difficulty with this Chakra— it is the seat of your ego, and to fully move past it, you will deal with self doubt and judgment, and any dishonesty that you are harboring. As the orange heat of the sacrum moves up, it will shift to yellow. Your mantra will give you the key to this step in awakening your energy. Your "gut" is where you feel pain, and where you must forgive yourself. Feel into any fear, pain, or anger that comes up for you as your yellow energy swirls up.

Your heart Chakra is waiting for you, and when you bring the energy into your chest, you will feel pure joy and love. Rich green love swirls within your heart cavity. Take the time to connect with your closest lovers and friends in this space. Smile and keep letting your words flow through you, swirling with the Chakra energy which will quickly move towards your throat, pushing up while you feel the expression of love and flow.

The Third Eye is the mystical home of the Pineal Gland, and as the energy moves up, you will feel pressure in your forehead and a lightness on your crown. This is where you can really breakthrough to Source and the Divine light of the Universe.

Many wise yogis experience astral travel and have multi-dimensional relationships with their spiritual guides and angels. After you master the visualization and do "the Work," you will find *Chakras* and meditation to be the gateway to true spiritual connection and to all of the richness that comes from *love*.

The first time you try a complex meditation, it may seem difficult, but the payoff is huge, and it gets very easy after a few times.

You were *meant* to meditate and connect with Source.

AFFIRMATION

I love and approve of myself.
I am grateful for my life.

AFTERWARD

BY SCOTT WATROUS

On the day I met Juliette, I really had no idea what the Universe was delivering me. In fact, I didn't really understand the world around me in the same way I do now. My LifesPath™ was still a mystery, and this beautifully exotic woman had yet to claim her place in my life.

She was a different kind of person and the impression lingered after the dinner meeting ended. We shared business cards, and when she said she had a book she was working on, I said what I always say: "Send me something to look at" and I went off into the evening.

What arrived via email was disarming. Raw. Brutally honest. Stream of consciousness flow without any editing. Kind of crazy! I told Jane something like, "No way I can make this make sense" and I turned over in my bed and slept.

And yet...Hmmmm. Something kept tugging at me. A little light inside blinked on, and I felt a pull to create something with Juliette. We talked, I imagined, Jane started to design, and the concept of LifesPath™ emerged and began to take on life.

The pages—reams!—of ideas and links continued to pour in from our new client, and I looked at them and drew inspiration, and saved everything.

Like all powerful unions, ours was rich with much potential, spawning opportunities and plans that often felt overwhelming. Juliette *is* flow. She moves and opens her energy as the Universe unveils it's options. She says "yes" and jumps. *Fast.* Corporate solutions, radio shows, articles, retreats... Infinite doors to walk through. Which one will open first?

I began to see Juliette in a very different light as our friendship grew. She is like a diamond—a pendant-shaped, perfectly-cut, crystal of magic and light that has been dragged through the mud a few times. Even though a shadow may pass through the stone, the light of truth burns through any patina that might obscure the message.

So, I learned—sometimes reluctantly. I accepted that I could be a student, and still be strong. I felt the joy of curiosity for the first time in years. I was inspired! And one day, zing! I got it. I knew. Juliette had the secret. When she said "I am ready to write a book!" I saw it in front of me, complete. The essence of my client—and friend— would find its way to the page, and I was called to be the scribe. Oh, how cool.

The "container" you hold in your hands is infused with mystery and magic, since Juliette is a seer and siren, comfortable in the realms of alchemy. Look closely, though, and you will find the message of transformation built on an unexpected platform—science. Really?? I knew there was something called "quantum physics" but without Juliette's spark...

Thank you for inviting me into your world, Juliette. This book *rocks!*

RESOURCES

Books

A Course in Miracles, by Helen Schucman
  (Foundation For Inner Peace)
A Practical Guide to Buddhist Meditation,
  by Paramananda
A Purpose Driven Life, by Rick Warren
A Return to Love: And The Gift of Change,
  by Marianne Williamson
Autobiography of A Yogi, by Yogananda
Conscious Creation, by Dee Wallace
*Creative Visualization: Use the Power of Your Imagination to
  Create What You Want in Your Life*, by Shakti Gawain
*Energy Medicine: Balancing Your Body's Energies for Optimal
  Health, Joy and Vitality*, by Donna Eden
Energy Secrets, by Alla Svirinskaya
Esoteric Buddhism, by A. P. Sinnet
Farm Sanctuary, by Gene Baur
*Grace: More Than We Deserve Greater Than We
  Imagine*, by Max Lucado
Human Being, by Dave Ellis
Inanna Returns, by V. S. Ferguson
Intuitive Thinking As A Spiritual Path, by Rudolf Steiner
Memories, Dreams and Reflections, by Carl Jung
Messages From Spirit, by Colette Baron-Reid
*Midnights with the Mystic: A Little Guide to Freedom and
  Bliss*, by Cheryl Simone with Sadhguru Jaggi Vasudev
Playing it Big, by Tara Mohr
Red, Hot & Holy, by Sara Beak

RESOURCES

Spiritually Incorrect Enlightenment (Part 1 of 3),
  by Jed McKenna
The Alchemist, by Paulo Coelho
The Celestine Prophesy, by James Redfield
The Collected Works of W.B. Yeats, by W.B. Yeats
The Cosmic Serpent, by Jeremy Narby
The Exquisite Risk, by Mark Nepo
The Fruitful Darkness, by Roshi Joan Halifax
The Healing Wisdom of Africa, by Malidoma Patrice Some
The Kybalion: The Definative Edition, by William
  Walker Atkinson (writing as Three Initiates)
The Mysts of Avalon, by Marion Zimmer Bradley
The Presence Process, by Michael Brown
The Secret, by Rhonda Byrne
The Soul of Money, by Lynne Twist
Success Through Stillness, by Russell Simmons with
  Chris Morrow
Traveling at the Speed of Love, by Sonja Choquette
You Can Heal Yourself, by Louise Hay
Wisdom Bowls, by Meredith Young-Sowers

Detox Retreat Centers
Hippocrates Health Institute, West Palm Beach, FL,
  www.hippocratesinst.org
The Tree of Life Rejuvenation Center, Patagonia, AZ,
  Dr. Gabriel Cousens, www.treeoflifecenterus.com

RESOURCES

Meditations and Yoga
Ashtanga Vinyasa Yoga
Bikram Yoga *(hot yoga)*
Hatha Yoga
Jivamukti Yoga *(Sharon Gannon works with many, including Sting and his wife Trudie)*
Kripalu Yoga
Kriya Yoga
Kundalini Yoga and meditations
Laughter Yoga
Nidra Yoga and meditations
Tantra Yoga
Transcendental meditation – Maharishi Mahesh Yogi *(remember the Beatles worked with him)*
Zen Yoga

Poets
Jalal al-Din Muhammad
Kahil Gibran, *The Beloved*
Maya Angelou, *A Brave and Startling Truth*
Oriah Mountain Dreamer
W.B. Yeats, *The Collected Works*

Resort Spas
Cal a Vie, Vista, CA
Canyon Ranch, Tuscon, AZ
The Crossings, Austin, TX
Edgar Cayce Health Care Center and Spa, Virginia Beach, VA
The Grand Del Mar, San Diego, CA
Green Valley Spa & Resort, St. George, UT
La Costa Resort Spa and the Chopra Center for Well Being, Carlsbad, CA
The Mayflower Inn and Spa, Washington, CT
Mii Amo, Sedona, AZ

RESOURCES

Miraval, Tuscon, AZ
Rancho Bernardo Inn & Spa, San Diego, CA
Salamander Resort, Middleburg, VA
Shambala Mountain Preserve, Heather Lakes, CO
Sagestone Spa at Red Mountain Resort, Ivans, UT
The Sanctuary Spa at Kiaweh Island Golf Resort,
  Charleston, SC
Sanivan Holistic Retreat & Spa, Hurleyville, NY
Turtle Bay Resort, Oahu, HI
Turtle Cove Spa, Mount Ida, AK
We Care Spa Juice Fasting and Spiritual Retreat,
  Palm Springs, CA

Spiritual Retreats
The Esalen Institute, Big Sur, CA
Kripalu Center for Yoga and Health, Stockbridge, MA
Omega Institute for Holistic Studies, Rhinebeck, NY
Upaya Zen Center, Santa Fe, NM

Teas and Healing
Arogya Holistic Healing, Westport, CT
(Fabulous place for tea and Chinese healing)

Websites
www.hayhouse.com
www.juliettetaylor.com
www.colettebaronreid.com
www.worldette.com
www.floweroflifepress.com

*Your Task is not to seek for love but merely to
seek and find all the barriers within yourself that
you have built against it.*

~A COURSE IN MIRACLES

NOTES

[1] Easwaran, Eknath (trans.), The Upanishads (Tomales, CA: The Blue Mountain Center of Meditation, 1987, 2007) pp. 268

[2] Robinson, James, M. ed., MacRae, George (trans.), The Nag Hammadi Library, revised edition (San Francisco: HarperCollins, 1990) ln. 200-204.

[3] http://www.hermeticsource.info/jalaluddin-rumi.html discussion Rumi and attribution of quotes. This quote is also credited to Schucman, Helen and Thetford, William, A Course In Miracles, Combined Vol. Third Ed., (Mill Valley, CA: Foundation For A Course in Miracles, 2007) pp. 338. Quite a bit of research was done to no avail to find the book in which this poem is listed. The poem is listed on the BBC website whom I trust did their research. http://www.bbc.co.uk/worldservice/learningenglish/movingwords/quotefeature/rumi.shtml

[4] http://www.hermeticsource.info/jalaluddin-rumi.html

[5] http://www.bashar.org/about/idesofmarch.html. Anka, Darryl, channeling Bashar

[6] Reminds me of the song by Van Morrison, In the Garden, No Guru, No Method, No Teacher album, July 1986 (Recorded in Sausalito, CA: Studio D at the Sausalito & Record Plant, 1985)

[7] Atkinson, William, Walker, writing as Three Initiates (Deslippe, Philip, ed.) The Kybalion (New York, NY: the Penguin Group, 2011) Originally published in 1908 with Seven Cosmic Laws completed in March 193. As not originally not copyrighted many authors have quoted directly.

[8] Merriam-Webster Dictionary

[9] http://quoteinvestigator.com/2012/07/18/best-not-seen/ "A nearly identical statement does appear in one of Keller's books. Intriguingly, the words were not credited to her. The book "The Story of My Life" by Helen Keller was published by 1905, and it included a letter dated June 8, 1891 from Keller to the Reverend Phillips Brooks. She was almost 11 years old when the letter was written, and it contained the following passage [HKAS]:

NOTES

> I used to wish that I could see pictures with my hands as I do statues, but now I do not often think about it because my dear Father has filled my mind with beautiful pictures, even of things I cannot see. If the light were not in your eyes, dear Mr. Brooks, you would understand better how happy your little Helen was when her teacher explained to her that the best and most beautiful things in the world cannot be seen nor even touched, but just felt in the heart. Every day I find out something which makes me glad.

An extraordinary woman named Anne Sullivan was Keller's teacher starting in 1887. So, the quotation originated with Sullivan instead of Keller; however, the young girl did embrace the thought it expressed. The statement evolved over time. For example, the phrase "felt in the heart" became "felt with the heart" in the modern version."

[10] Eveleth Rose. "There are 37.2 trillion Cells in your Body," The Smithsonian.com (October 24, 2013)

[11] Myss, Caroline. "Entering the Castle: Exploring Your Mystical Experience of God," www.myss.com: Caroline Myss News (October 7, 2007).

[12] Lincoln, Don. "The Good Vibrations of Quantum Field Theories." Nova blogs, physics. pbs.org (August 5, 2013)

[13] Adyashanti, The End of your World: Uncensored Straight Talk on the Nature of Enlightenment. (Boulder, Co: Sounds True 2008)

[14] Wallace, Dee. Trademarked August 16, 2011

[15] Chopra, Deepak. "Harness Your Mind's Power to Heal and Transform." chopra.com. http://www.chopra.com/ccl/harness-your-minds-power-to-heal-and-transform.

[16] Byrne, Rhonda. The Secret. (Hillsboro, OR: Beyond Words Publishing, 2006) pp. 47-57

[17] Young-Sowers, Meredith. Spirit Heals. (Novato, CA: New World Library, 2007) pp. 8-9

ABOUT THE AUTHOR

Juliette is a modern day shaman, a "shamanista," living a real life filled with magic and love—a life she co-created with the Universe.

She is a Certified Life Coach, motivational speaker, writer and the creator of the LifesPath™ process to finding health, happiness, and love. Her method is unique, powerful, and rooted firmly in the tradition of her Huguenot and Shaman forebears—witches and wise women, Shamans and blacksmiths, their DNA wired tightly with Juliette's. She has guided hundreds of clients to breakthrough their blocks, dispel limiting beliefs, and find their core strength to live lives they absolutely love.

Her practice fuses body, mind, and spirit through focused attention and visualization, meditation, daily spiritual rituals, and a plant-based diet.

Juliette specializes in guiding you to let go of fear, and challenges the deep-rooted beliefs holding you back, exploring your spiritual awakenings, and teaching you to exercise and eat intuitively so you, too, can live a life you love.

Her diverse corporate experience spans economic development, real estate, building start-ups, total staff management, fundraising for social profits, corporate sales development, wellness, and food sustainability. She formerly worked as COO of Wholesome Wave Foundation Charitable Ventures. She holds a BA from the University of California Irvine and is working on her Masters in Metaphysics from the American Institute of Holistic Theology.